Georgia
Simply Beautiful

Photography by Robb Helfrick and James Randklev

FARCOUNTRY
PRESS

ABOVE: Atop Stone Mountain.
ROBB HELFRICK

RIGHT: Shrimp boats on the Darien River.
ROBB HELFRICK

TITLE PAGE: The Tallulah River in the Blue Ridge Mountains.
JAMES RANDKLEV

FRONT COVER: Banks Lake National Wildlife Refuge.
ROBB HELFRICK

BACK COVER: Golden Isle sunrise.
JAMES RANDKLEV

ENDPAPERS AND COVER BACKGROUND: Stone Mountain.
ROBB HELFRICK

ISBN 1-56037-202-8

© 2002 Farcountry Press

Photographs © by individual photographers as credited

This book may not be reproduced in whole or in part by any means (with the exception of short quotes for the purpose of review) without permission of the publisher. For more information on our books call or write: Farcountry Press, P.O. Box 5630, Helena, MT 59604, (406) 443-2842 or (800) 654-1105, or visit our website: www.montanamagazine.com

Created, designed and published in the USA. Printed in China.

I arrived in Georgia at the age of twenty-one, lured by the promise of Atlanta, a prospering city far from my small town roots. For my first few years I was a city and suburb dweller, and I knew little of the treasures that awaited in the marshes and mountains of my adopted state.

My eyes were opened when I took my first trip to Savannah. The journey to Georgia's birthplace was a welcome respite from fast paced, big business Atlanta. Savannah had verdant squares shaded by the twisted forms of live oak trees that seemed to come alive when the Spanish moss swayed in a sultry southern breeze. The pace of life was much to my liking, for it was easy to amble and wander and slow down a bit. The history and elegance of the city were equally captivating. Its colorful past was filled with stories of successful cotton merchants who left a legacy of grand architecture—a legacy saved a hundred dred years later by a group of determined ladies who laid the groundwork for the city's historic preservation. Savannah was flaunting its riot of spring hues when I first arrived, azaleas colored every square, and flowering dogwoods framed the doorways of stately residences. I was caught in the spell of this mysterious and beautiful southern city, and to this day I can't stay away too long from my favorite place in Georgia.

It wasn't long after I discovered Savannah that I became a photographer. I found myself in the fortunate position of earning a living in a workplace that stretched from the Atlantic Ocean to the Appalachian Mountains. My office was Georgia. One of my first assignments, one that gave me great respect for the depth and diversity of my new home, involved working with Georgia's State Parks and Historic Sites. In the process of photographing every forest, lake, and historic home in the park system, I slowly began to memorize the back roads of Georgia, and feel the rhythm of the seasons as they provided distinct color and light on the landscape. I fell into the ritual of traveling a predictable and pleasurable seasonal trail through the state year after year. In October, rugged Cloudland Canyon was the locale for autumn colors, in early May spectacular Tallulah Gorge displayed multiple shades of green foliage with the coming of spring. Wintertime was a quiet season to visit and photograph Jekyll or Ossabaw Island along the coast, and summer was spent close to home at Red Top Mountain, where the whitetail deer roam.

Sunset over St. Simons Lighthouse, St. Simons Island.
ROBB HELFRICK

Georgia has an endless variety of scenic wonders and natural habitats that make it a unique place to live and work. The chain of barrier islands along the Atlantic coast, the Golden Isles, is unrivaled on the eastern seaboard for its untamed natural beauty. Stone Mountain towers over the piedmont, just east of Atlanta, and impresses with its sheer size and granite might. The Appalachian Mountains range across Georgia's northern reaches and, hidden in their hardwood forests and on top their ancient summits, are an amazing medley of plants and animals. The famed Okefenokee Swamp, land of alligator and cypress, black water and trembling earth, has captured the imagination of many who have canoed silently over its reflective surface. These distinct Georgia places have endured, thanks to the efforts of many dedicated individuals and organizations who protect them with a gentle guiding hand. Such people and groups strive to preserve these last vestiges of wilderness not only as a reminder of what Georgia once was, but also with hope for what it will be in the years to come.

R.H.

*G*eorgia—land of gentle spirit.

Georgia first came to me in the words of *Gone with the Wind* and Sidney Lanier's poems, such as "The Marshes of Glynn." This is a state steeped in history with a landscape rich in contrast and spirit. I have long traveled this region that is covered in pine forests that seem to go on forever like an undulating sea of green. Centuries-old oaks cloaked in Spanish moss stand silent with memories of a bygone era. The Appalachians, lush with mixed hardwoods and countless waterfalls, keep me spellbound with their beauty. If that weren't enough, the coastal plains with crystalline springs and one of the greatest primordial swamps, the Okefenokee, inspire me. Georgia's barrier islands impress me the most, just for their raw beauty and remoteness. These Golden Isles were once inhabited by Guale Indians, who hunted and fished these tidal marshes thousands of years ago. To this day there are remnants of plantation sites that reflect a time of great wealth as well as hardship. Walking the solitary beaches bordered by windswept dunes covered in sea oats inspires me to capture a landscape unlike any other I have experienced.

Georgia seduces my photographic vision. Whether it is the dramatic granite outcrops of Stone Mountain and Brasstown Bald, or the delicate white blossoms of water lilies in Okefenokee Swamp, or something as simple as scattered autumn leaves along a streambed in Cloudland Canyon, some facet always captivates my attention. I never tire of Georgia's natural wonders, whether on a grand scale or intimate in detail.

My first visit to the Peach State was like a handshake with a new friend. Subsequent visits had made me feel like I had a second home to enjoy. I realize, though, that in addition to Georgia's back roads, rivers, swamps, islands, and mountains, the people of this charming state are its greatest resource. Southern hospitality is alive and well here, and folks really care about their land and each other. So many times I have been helped with directions when I was lost on some tiny dirt road looking for a waterfall or hidden nature preserve. Like so many people in our great country, Georgians appreciate their natural and historic sites and work hard to protect what they have for future generations to enjoy.

Georgia will continue to inspire and lure me to where people and nature exist in a harmony that brings joy to all.

Wild and Scenic Chattooga River.
JAMES RANDKLEV

ABOVE: Hay House in Macon, open for tours, was built in 1855 and today looks as it was decorated by the 1925 purchasers, Mr. and Mrs. Park Lee Hay.
ROBB HELFRICK

FACING PAGE: Live oaks, like this one along Cumberland Island's Brickhill River, often are beautifully draped with Spanish moss.
JAMES RANDKLEV

RIGHT: Fog nourishes the ferns of Hog Pen Gap, Chattahoochee National Forest.
JAMES RANDKLEV

BELOW: One of President Jimmy Carter's boyhood homes in Plains' Jimmy Carter National Historic Site.
ROBB HELFRICK

ABOVE: River Street was Savannah's cotton warehouse district, but today its converted buildings house restaurants and shops.
ROBB HELFRICK

FACING PAGE: Autumn reflections paint Holly Creek in the Cohutta Wilderness.
JAMES RANDKLEV

FOLLOWING PAGES: Cypress trees model their fall foliage in George L. Smith II State Park northwest of Savannah.
JAMES RANDKLEV

ABOVE: In George T. Bagby State Park, where recreation opportunities range from golfing an award-winning eighteen-hole course, to water skiing, to wildlife watching along the nature trail.
JAMES RANDKLEV

FACING PAGE: Dogwood trees, delicately flowering to announce spring, are native to North America.
JAMES RANDKLEV

ABOVE: Oak Hill, in Rome, was a plantation home built in 1847, and now sits on the campus of Berry College, which grew from education efforts by Martha Berry, inheritor of the mansion.
ROBB HELFRICK

RIGHT: Near Lake Seminole, skeletons of trees rise from the water that overran them.
JAMES RANDKLEV

LEFT: The double-barrelled cannon in Athens' City Hall Plaza is an experiment that failed the one time it was fired, after being made here during the Civil War.
ROBB HELFRICK

BELOW: The cool green of ferns along the Chattooga River in Rabun County.
JAMES RANDKLEV

FACING PAGE: Confederate soldiers survived bombardment by ironclad boats in these earthen bunkers at Fort McAllister near Richmond Hill.
ROBB HELFRICK

ABOVE: Stone Mountain's gigantic granite dome bears sculptures of Jefferson Davis, Robert E. Lee, and Thomas "Stonewall" Jackson—its bulk dwarfing the nine-story-tall figures.
JAMES RANDKLEV

FACING PAGE: Looking from Springer Mountain into Amicalola Falls State Park.
JAMES RANDKLEV

ABOVE: Starr's Mill belongs to Fayetteville and centers a public park
open for fishing and picnicking.
ROBB HELFRICK

RIGHT: Red Clover and purple vetch adorn a Coffee County field.
JAMES RANDKLEV

ABOVE: Toccoa Falls, taller than Niagara Falls, was given that name meaning "beautiful" by Native Americans.
JAMES RANDKLEV

RIGHT: Lake Winfield Scott, headwaters of Cooper Creek, offers boating and swimming, and is surrounded by hiking trails.
ROBB HELFRICK

ABOVE: Cypress's heartwood is very resistant to decaying, so it has been used to build docks, boats, and bridges.
JAMES RANDKLEV

FACING PAGE: A calico crab among clamshells washed up during low tide.
JAMES RANDKLEV

Peach orchards provide spring beauty
as well as the Peach State's nickname.
ROBB HELFRICK

ABOVE: Thirty hours of Union bombardment in 1862 left projectiles that are still in the thick masonry walls of Fort Pulaski, now a national monument.
ROBB HELFRICK

LEFT: Ebenezer Creek near Savannah is a national attraction to sea kayakers.
JAMES RANDKLEV

ABOVE: Jekyll Island Club was the private domain of millionaire industrialists in the late 19th century, when they owned the sea island that is now one of Georgia's most popular resorts.
ROBB HELFRICK

FACING PAGE: A tidal stream wanders across Sapelo Island, another of Georgia's Golden Isles in the Atlantic.
JAMES RANDKLEV

ABOVE: Milledgeville was capital of Georgia beginning in 1807, and state governors lived in this mansion between 1839 and 1869.
ROBB HELFRICK

LEFT: Mosquito Creek on Little St. Simons Island.
JAMES RANDKLEV

ABOVE: Flat Shoals Creek near West Point.
JAMES RANDKLEV

RIGHT: Tift Park in Albany honors the memory of Nelson Tift,
one of the city's first residents in 1836.
ROBB HELFRICK

FOLLOWING PAGES: Purple twilight splendor below Black Rock
Mountain in the Appalachians.
JAMES RANDKLEV

ABOVE: Just a short distance from the Savannah River, the Cotton & Naval Stores Exchange in Savannah once was a court where King Cotton ruled.
ROBB HELFRICK

FACING PAGE: Providence Canyon State Park, south of Columbus, is often called "Georgia's Little Grand Canyon."
ROBB HELFRICK

ABOVE: Bird's foot violets rise from oak leaves in
Black Rock Mountain State Park.
JAMES RANDKLEV

RIGHT: Allatoona Lake settles in for a winter night.
ROBB HELFRICK

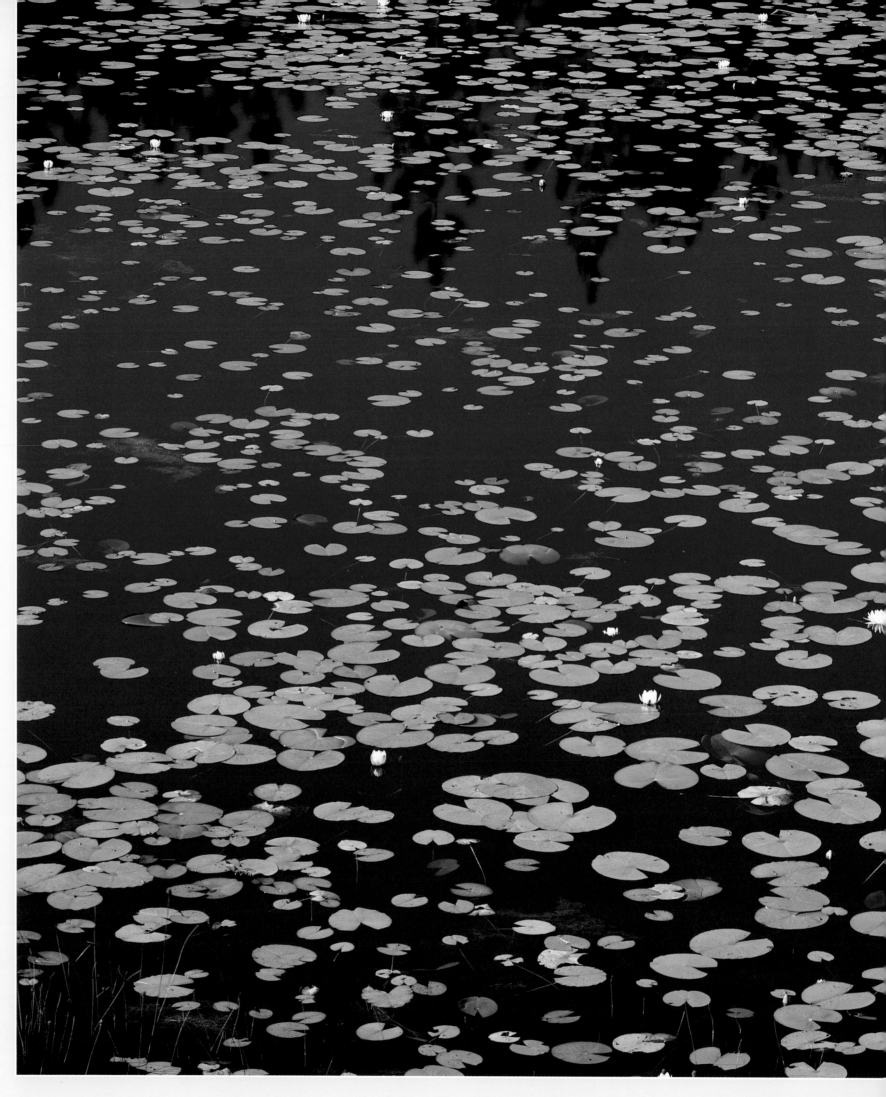

LEFT: Lily pads offer a contrast atop Okefenokee Swamp's black water.
JAMES RANDKLEV

BELOW: The Altamaha River, the southeastern United States' largest unaltered river, makes its way through cypress swamps on the coastal plain.
JAMES RANDKLEV

ABOVE: Apples in every color and flavor, after the harvest near Ellijay.
ROBB HELFRICK

RIGHT: James H. Floyd State Park in Georgia's northwestern corner.
JAMES RANDKLEV

LEFT: Night time is a busy time on certain beaches.
JAMES RANDKLEV

BELOW: A white-tailed deer sentry on the alert.
ROBB HELFRICK

FACING PAGE: Cumberland Island in the morning fog.
JAMES RANDKLEV

ABOVE: Native flame azaleas and bracken ferns flourish in Callaway Gardens near Pine Mountain, which also includes miles of scenic drives.

JAMES RANDKLEV

RIGHT: Barnsley Gardens at Adairsville was an estate named Woodlands built in the late 1830s that survived the Civil War only to burn later.

ROBB HELFRICK

ABOVE: Etowah Mounds State Historic Site was an Indian settlement around 1000 A.D.
ROBB HELFRICK

FACING PAGE: Palmettos and live oaks make an intriguing study in green.
JAMES RANDKLEV

ABOVE: Orderly rows of a youthful pine forest planting.
JAMES RANDKLEV

RIGHT: Gordonia-Altamaha State Park near Reidsville.
ROBB HELFRICK

ABOVE: Atlanta, powerhouse city of the New South.
ROBB HELFRICK

FACING PAGE: Cloudland Canyon State Park, near Chickamauga,
holds the upper waters of Daniel Creek.
JAMES RANDKLEV

ABOVE: The sculptor's art shaped a realistic sharpshooter at Chickamauga National Battlefield.
ROBB HELFRICK

RIGHT: Crescent House in Valdosta holds one column for each of the original thirteen British colonies.
JAMES RANDKLEV

ABOVE: Little White House State Historic Site at Warm Springs preserves the home Franklin Roosevelt built here in 1932, and where he died in 1945.
ROBB HELFRICK

LEFT: Pecan still life.
ROBB HELFRICK

FACING PAGE: Macon's cherry blossom festival is one of the largest in the United States.
JAMES RANDKLEV

ABOVE: Near Clayton on north Georgia's scenic Highway 76.
JAMES RANDKLEV

RIGHT: The rugged Cloudland Canyon State Park.
ROBB HELFRICK

ABOVE: Just waiting patiently, an alligator in Okefenokee.
JAMES RANDKLEV

LEFT: Tupelo trees along the Ogeechee River.
JAMES RANDKLEV

LEFT: A monument at Washington portrays a young Confederate soldier.
ROBB HELFRICK

BELOW: Pine cones and the leaves of grape, dogwood, and gum trees weave a forest-floor carpet.
JAMES RANDKLEV

FACING PAGE: Sourwood trees along Unicoi Lake in the Chattahoochee National Forest.
JAMES RANDKLEV

ABOVE: Cypress line Banks Lake.
ROBB HELFRICK

FACING PAGE: Fantastically eroded limestone formations of Rock Town on Pigeon Mountain.
JAMES RANDKLEV

FOLLOWING PAGES: Boat tours and canoeing are available on the Suwanee River in Okefenokee Swamp near the Florida border.
JAMES RANDKLEV

ABOVE: Savannah's Forsyth Park, dating from 1851, includes a fountain resembling the one in Paris's Place de la Concorde.
ROBB HELFRICK

LEFT: Rising to 4,784 feet, Brasstown Bald is Georgia's highest point.
ROBB HELFRICK

BELOW: Sand dollars are flat cousins of pincushion-like sea urchins.
JAMES RANDKLEV

ABOVE: Starfish decorate Georgia ocean beaches during low tide.
ROBB HELFRICK

RIGHT: An Ossabaw Island marsh reflects day's end.
ROBB HELFRICK

ABOVE: Minnehaha Falls.

JAMES RANDKLEV

LEFT: Saltilla River, Georgia's largest blackwater system.

JAMES RANDKLEV

ABOVE: Azaleas grace one of Callaway Gardens' forest pathways as they have since the 1930s.
JAMES RANDKLEV

RIGHT: The Medical College of Georgia, Augusta.
ROBB HELFRICK

LEFT: Richard Russell Highway offers fourteen miles of marvelous scenic views in the Blairsville area.

ROBB HELFRICK

BELOW: The Lapham-Patterson House State Historic Site in Thomasville shows an intriguing 1884 "winter cottage" that has no two rooms the same shape—and no room with four exactly square corners.

JAMES RANDKLEV

Live oaks are popular shade trees in Georgia.

JAMES RANDKLEV

LEFT: Fort Pulaski from the air shows its unusual pentagonal shape.
ROBB HELFRICK

BELOW: Radium Springs at Albany.
ROBB HELFRICK

FACING PAGE: Godby Springs along Spring Creek in Seminole County.
JAMES RANDKLEV

ABOVE: A meadow of cinnamon ferns on St Simons Island, one of the Golden Isles.
JAMES RANDKLEV

LEFT: A new crop of Georgia peaches is coming on in Fort Valley.
ROBB HELFRICK

LEFT: Wild horses are one of the treats for Cumberland Island visitors.
JAMES RANDKLEV

BELOW: In Amicalola Falls State Park near Dahlonega.
JAMES RANDKLEV

FACING PAGE: The dome of the Georgia State Capitol in Atlanta shines with gold leaf from ore mined in the state.
JAMES RANDKLEV

ABOVE: On Little St. Simons Island, where yellow pines and palmettos end and spartina grass begins.
JAMES RANDKLEV

LEFT: Looking down into Tallulah Gorge.
ROBB HELFRICK

ABOVE: Near Perry.
ROBB HELFRICK

FACING PAGE: Depression pool with lichen in Heggies Rock's granite outcrop.
JAMES RANDKLEV

ABOVE: At West Point, a friendly setting for friends to sit 'n' rock.
JAMES RANDKLEV

FACING PAGE: A foggy day in Okefenokee country.
ROBB HELFRICK

ABOVE: The Windsor Hotel in Americus was built in 1892
and refurbished in Victorian style in 1991.

ROBB HELFRICK

LEFT: Raven Cliffs Scenic Area shows the gentle, rounded profiles
of the Appalachian Mountains.

JAMES RANDKLEV

ABOVE: The Rose Garden section of State Botanical Gardens
of Georgia, in Athens.
ROBB HELFRICK

FACING PAGE: An ancient live oak on Wassaw Island.
JAMES RANDKLEV

ABOVE: Great blue herons are at home in Savannah National Wildlife Refuge.
ROBB HELFRICK

LEFT: Near Cartersville, river grass along the Etowah River.
ROBB HELFRICK

ABOVE: And just *who* might you be? Near Byron.
ROBB HELFRICK

FACING PAGE: Lake Conasauga on the western edge of Georgia's
Blue Ridge Mountains.
JAMES RANDKLEV

ABOVE: Andersonville National Historic Site, site of a prison camp that the Confederacy could ill afford to run, today honors all who ever have been prisoners of war in the defense of the nation. Seen here is the Minnesota memorial.
ROBB HELFRICK

RIGHT: Billys Lake in Stephen C. Foster State Park.
JAMES RANDKLEV

LEFT: Dockery Lake in northern Georgia.
ROBB HELFRICK

BELOW: Harvest time at Burt's Pumpkin Farm near Amicalola Falls State Park.
ROBB HELFRICK

RIGHT: Water lilies.
JAMES RANDKLEV

FACING PAGE: Escowee River Falls' gentle cascades.
JAMES RANDKLEV

BELOW: Auchumpkee Covered Bridge is in Upson County.
ROBB HELFRICK

ABOVE: Jekyll Island sunrise and surf.
ROBB HELFRICK

FACING PAGE: The St. Johns River flows through northern Georgia.
JAMES RANDKLEV

ABOVE: Lichen-covered oak branches on Cumberland Island.
JAMES RANDKLEV

LEFT: The gristmill at Berry College in Rome has one of the world's largest mill wheels, measuring forty-two feet in diameter.
ROBB HELFRICK

ABOVE: Augusta's Sacred Heart Cultural Center is a former Catholic church built in 1900.
ROBB HELFRICK

FACING PAGE: At Fort McAllister in December 1864 was the last time General William Tecumseh Sherman ordered artillery fire during the Civil War.
ROBB HELFRICK

Bobby Brown State Park, a quiet refuge on Clarks Hill Reservoir, holds
the largest man-made lake east of the Mississippi, and its name honors
Lt. Robert T. Brown, who died in U.S. Navy service during World War II.
ROBB HELFRICK

120